Escape Poverty

Destiny S. Harris

...

. . .

Copyright

. . .

...

A Gift For You

Thank you for taking the time to read this book. As a token of my appreciation, here is a gift to you.

I give away free books daily. Here's how to get your free books today:

Step 1: Visit amazon.com/author/destinyharris

Step 2: Filter books by "Price: Low to High"

Step 3: Download available free eBooks

. . .

. . .

Table of Contents

. . .

...

Quick Bit

Thank you for taking the time to read this book.

My hope is that you leave at least 1% better than before you read this book and walk away with at least one takeaway.

I'd like to graciously ask that you help me by leaving a <u>review</u> of this book; your feedback helps me write better books and helps others get a glimpse of the book.

With Kindness,
Destiny

. . .

...

The Bottom

I still remember the days I made a couple hundred dollars per month. For some people, this is enough; for many in a third-world country, this is plenty. But in most parts of America, this doesn't cut it.

What did I do to shift my financial situation?

A few things:

1. Exposure
2. Self-Education
3. Action

. . .

. . .

1: Exposure

If you don't know you can do better, you won't. A person who always dates scrubs and only knows scrubs will likely only date more scrubs; they don't know anyone out there is better because they've never been exposed.

Expose yourself to surroundings, places, people, and opportunities that are foreign to you. How do you access these? Research, networking, and effort.

Everyone will usually come in contact with someone or something with resources. Seize these moments and embrace the opportunity. It's the only way to grow.

My family didn't come from money, but my father worked around and with millionaires and billionaires, which exposed me to a higher lifestyle.

. . .

. . .

2: Self-Education

My parents did a peculiar thing and had us read personal finance at the dinner table. No one in my family was good with money, yet we read personal finance books at the dinner table, which shifted my entire financial trajectory.

I have never stopped reading personal finance books and am still studying them.

With more knowledge comes the opportunity to do better. How do I know? Because I used to be broke, and now I'm not. How did this change happen? Financial education. I still read today because I refuse to allow ignorance to overtake my financial destiny.

. . .

. . .

3: Action

With more knowledge comes responsibility.

As I have acquired more financial knowledge, one thing is sure: if I don't act, my situation won't improve.

How can one improve?

Consistent action.

1. Exposure yourself to people with money.
2. Read books.
3. Act.

If you're broke, what you're doing today obviously isn't working. You need to shift your paradigm and habits to yield a different result.

Are you ready? The sooner you're ready to embrace change (which is often paired with pain/discomfort), the sooner you can transform your financial situation.

Four basics you should always do with your money:

1. Live below your means. Spend less than you earn.

2. Invest a minimum of 10% of your income.

3. Continuously self-educate yourself. Read books on personal finance.

4. Continuously increase your income.

. . .

. . .

Thank You For Reading

Thank you for reading this book.

Stay loved, blessed, lucky, favored, aware, joyous, enlightened, and committed to bettering yourself.

. . .

. . .

The End.

. . .

. . .

About Destiny S. Harris

Destiny S. Harris' goal is to positively inspire, cultivate, elevate, and educate the minds of individuals across the globe through her writing.

Creating (whether books, courses, articles, poetry, or music) has always been Destiny's thing, not to mention health & fitness and all things entrepreneurial.

Destiny published her first book, "Beauty Secrets for Girls," at age 11 and her second book, "Don't Wait Until It's Too Late," at age 12.

Destiny obtained three degrees in Psychology, Political Science, & Women's Studies. She also started her own music teaching business at the age of 14, which she led for over ten years. In addition, she has been teaching academic, career, and personal development topics to thousands of students and readers since 2004.

Outside of writing, Destiny loves and enjoys many activities: reading, weightlifting, walking, biking, traveling, football (and sports in general), dogs, animals, food, classic movies, quality and new experiences, mountain and ocean views, sleeping, plants, and nature.

Check out her work, leave a review, share your thoughts with your friends and family, and participate in a movement: **Serving others through self-education (books).**

Complete the Steps To Get Free eBooks:

Step 1: Go to amazon.com/author/destinyharris

Step 2: Filter books by "Price: Low to High"

Step 3: Download available free books

. . .

. . .

Connect W/ Destiny S. Harris

Please reach out and stay in touch. Start a conversation today @ destinyh.com

. . .

. . .

Free Gifts!

Access courses & free eBooks at the link below:

destinyh.com

. . .

Please Leave A Review

If this book impacts you in some way, please let me know by dropping a review on it.

I write better books with **your** input.

...

Tell Me What You Want

I've written many books, but if you don't see what you're looking for or need, get in touch with me via my website, articles, comments, or reviews, and let me know what you're looking for so I can create it for you. I'm here to serve.

Destiny

. . .

. . .